CENGAGE Learning

Novels for Students, Volume 12

Staff

Editor: Elizabeth Thomason.

Contributing Editors: Reginald Carlton, Anne Marie Hacht, Michael L. LaBlanc, Ira Mark Milne, Jennifer Smith.

Managing Editor, Content: Dwayne D. Hayes.

Managing Editor, Product: David Galens.

Publisher, Literature Product: Mark Scott.

Literature Content Capture: Joyce Nakamura, *Managing Editor*. Sara Constantakis, *Editor*.

Research: Victoria B. Cariappa, *Research Manager*. Cheryl Warnock, *Research Specialist*. Tamara Nott, Tracie A. Richardson, *Research Associates*. Nicodemus Ford, Sarah Genik, Timothy Lehnerer, Ron Morelli, *Research Assistants*.

Permissions: Maria Franklin, *Permissions*

Manager. Jacqueline Jones, Julie Juengling, *Permissions Assistants*.

Manufacturing: Mary Beth Trimper, *Manager, Composition and Electronic Prepress*. Evi Seoud, *Assistant Manager, Composition Purchasing and Electronic Prepress*. Stacy Melson, *Buyer*.

Imaging and Multimedia Content Team: Barbara Yarrow, *Manager*. Randy Bassett, *Imaging Supervisor*. Robert Duncan, Dan Newell, *Imaging Specialists*. Pamela A. Reed, *Imaging Coordinator*. Leitha Etheridge-Sims, Mary Grimes, David G. Oblender, *Image Catalogers*. Robyn V. Young, *Project Manager*. Dean Dauphinais, *Senior Image Editor*. Kelly A. Quin, *Image Editor*.

Product Design Team: Kenn Zorn, *Product Design Manager*. Pamela A. E. Galbreath, *Senior Art Director*. Michael Logusz, *Graphic Artist*.

Copyright © 2001
Gale Group
27500 Drake Rd.
Farmington Hills, MI 48331-3535

ISBN 0-7876-4895-7
ISSN 1094-3552

Printed in the United States of America.
10 9 8 7 6 5 4 3 2 1

Mrs. Dalloway

Virginia Woolf

1925

Introduction

Virginia Woolf's *Mrs. Dalloway*, published in 1925, was a bestseller both in Britain and the United States despite its departure from typical novelistic style. *Mrs. Dalloway* and Woolf's subsequent book, *To the Lighthouse*, have generated the most critical attention and are the most widely studied of Woolf's novels.

The action of *Mrs. Dalloway* takes place during a single day in June 1923 in London, England. This unusual organizational strategy creates a special problem for the novelist: how to craft characters deep enough to be realistic while treating only one day in their lives. Woolf solved this problem with what she called a "tunneling" technique, referring to the way her characters remember their pasts. In experiencing these characters' recollections, readers derive for themselves a sense of background and history to characters that, otherwise, a narrator would have had to provide.

In a sense, *Mrs. Dalloway* is a novel without a plot. Instead of creating major situations between characters to push the story forward, Woolf moved her narrative by following the passing hours of a day. The book is composed of movements from one character to another, or of movements from the internal thoughts of one character to the internal thoughts of another.

Mrs. Dalloway has been called a *flâneur* novel, which means it depicts people walking about a city. (*Flâneur* is the French word for a person who enjoys walking around a city often with no other purpose than to see the sights.) The book, as is typi of the *flâneur* novel, makes the city, its parks, and its streets as interesting as the characters who inhabit them.

Clarissa Dalloway's party, which is the culminating event of the book, ties the narrative together by gathering the group of friends Clarissa thinks about throughout her day. It also concludes the secondary story of the book, the story of Septimus Warren Smith, by having Dr. Bradshaw arrive at the party and mention that one of his patients committed suicide that day.

The book's major competing themes are isolation and community, or the possibilities and limits of communicativeness, as evidenced by Clarissa's abiding sense of being alone and by her social skills, which bring people together at her parties.

Author Biography

Virginia Woolf was born in 1882 in London, England. She was the daughter of Leslie Stephen, an eminent man of letters, and Julia Prinsep Jackson Duckworth. The Stephen-Duckworth household had many children and was financially secure. Woolf had free rein of her father's extensive library, and was able to educate herself thoroughly.

Woolf was brought up in a scholarly and creative environment. Following her father's death in 1904, Woolf and three of her siblings moved to a house in Bloomsbury (a neighborhood of London) where they cultivated a similar atmosphere. Woolf began writing and publishing at this time, mostly literary criticism, and not yet fiction. In 1907, when her sister Vanessa (a painter) married art critic Clive Bell, Woolf and a brother moved to another house. The writers, intellectuals, and artists who met at this house played central and pivotal roles in British early twentieth-century intellectual and cultural history. They were known as the Bloomsbury group, and they espoused a number of common views; for example, most were pacifists. To Woolf, questions of gender, gender difference, and sexuality became extremely important. She was interested in the commonalties of men and women as well as their differences, and she argued that artists had androgynous minds.

Woolf began publishing fiction in 1915, and it

was with her third novel (*Jacob's Room*, 1922) that she began to show maturity as a writer. *Mrs. Dalloway*, her fourth novel, is evidence of the consol-idation of a major and rare fictional talent. Woolf went on to publish more novels, and these, together with her extensive non-fiction publications, amount to one of the most distinguished bodies of literature in the English language.

Virginia Woolf (then Virginia Stephen) married Leonard Woolf, a politician and writer, in 1912. Despite the success of her marriage and publishing career, she suffered bouts of mental disequilibrium throughout her life, periods of madness or nearmadness that terrified her. After each recovery she was haunted by the thought that the next time she might not return to sanity. This fear, along with the depressing events of WWII, finally proved too much for her to bear. Convinced that Hitler's forces would prevail, and mired in a period of depression, Woolf committed suicide by drowning in Lewes, Sussex, England on March 28, 1941.

Section 1

Mrs. Dalloway begins with a sentence that is also its first paragraph: "Mrs. Dalloway said she would buy the flowers herself." The second para mentions that "doors would be taken off their hinges," so it is possible to determine that there will be an event at Mrs. Dalloway's house that day, and that Clarissa is going out to buy flowers for the affair.

Setting out for her purchases reminds Clarissa of how she used to "burst open the French doors" at Bourton, the country house of her youth. She also remembers, in connection with Bourton, a close friend of her youth, Peter Walsh. On the way to the flower shop, Clarissa runs into another old friend, Hugh Whitbread. Section 1 ends when, from within the flower shop, Clarissa hears the loud sound of a car backfiring.

Section 2

The sound of the car backfiring facilitates a shift in which character's point of view dominates the narrative. Septimus Warren Smith, a major character, is introduced in this way. Septimus and his wife, Lucrezia, are walking along the street where the flower shop and backfiring car are located, on their way to Regent's Park. Septimus is mentally disturbed, a young man who has come back from the First World War (WWI) suffering from shell shock. The public sounds of the car backfiring and an "aeroplane" roaring overhead allowed Woolf to register, besides the points of view of Septimus and Lucrezia, the points of view of a number of passersby who are not major characters in the book.

Section 3

Clarissa arrives home, having ordered the flowers. She finds that her husband has been invited to lunch at Lady Bruton's. She decides to mend the dress that she will be wearing that evening at her party. Once again, she thinks about various people, things, and her past, and so the novel builds a sense of her character and what issues are pertinent to her. One significant person she thinks about is Sally Seton, a close friend of her youth, with whom she had been in love.

Peter Walsh drops by unexpectedly; Clarissa is not aware that he has returned to London from India. With this visit, the past enters the present forcibly, as the man who preoccupied Clarissa's thoughts that morning appears in person. She invites him to her party.

Section 4

Section 4 follows Peter Walsh on an amble

about town after he leaves Clarissa's house. He also thinks about their past, how he loved Clarissa, and how he found fault with her. He thinks about her party that evening and her parties in general. He ends up in Regent's Park (where the book left Septimus and Lucrezia), where he falls into a slumber on a bench.

Section 5

This section is very brief and appears to record Peter's sleeping dream in which a figure referred to as the "solitary traveller" is the principal protagonist.

Section 6

Peter awakes and ruminates over Clarissa, Bourton, Sally Seton and Richard Dalloway: how he loved Clarissa, had been jealous of Richard, had been close to Sally, and had criticized Clarissa.

Section 7

Section 7 is the lengthiest of the eight sections of the U.S. edition of the novel (the first published British edition had twelve sections). The location of Regent's Park, where Peter has been snoozing, and where Septimus and his wife have been sitting on a bench, facilitates a shift from Peter Walsh back to the troubled young couple. They are waiting for their noon appointment with Dr. Bradshaw. Much of this section is Septimus' point of view, and so the reader gets a glimpse into the workings of his distressed and strained mind. Lucrezia agonizes about her husband's condition and how people must see that all is not well with them.

Moving back to Peter, the reader finds that he is still musing about the past, how Clarissa is a snob who loves high society, and how her snobbery and love of comfort led her to choose Richard Dalloway over himself for a husband.

As Peter leaves the park, he walks by an old vagrant woman singing a song; Septimus and Lucrezia pass the same woman at the same time, and so the narrative shifts to the couple again. At this point, Septimus's history is presented: how he came to London showing great promise, but returned from the war traumatized. From Lucrezia's thoughts, the reader learns that Septimus has threatened to kill himself.

At noon, Big Ben strikes. Clarissa hears it at home while she is mending her dress, and Septimus and his wife arrive for their appointment at the establishment of Sir William Bradshaw. Bradshaw promises to arrange for Septimus to go to a rest home because he sees that the young man's condition is grave and advanced. The narrative then dis doctors such as Bradshaw, questioning the methods and assumptions by which they diagnose and practice.

The scene now shifts to Richard Dalloway, at his lunch with Lady Bruton. Hugh Whitbread has also been invited. Lady Bruton wants their help revising a letter she has composed to the *Times* about the need for emigration; Hugh quickly edits it after lunch.

The two men leave Lady Bruton's. Hugh stops to buy a gift for his wife and Richard decides to buy and deliver flowers to Clarissa. Clarissa is pleased and informs Richard that their daughter, Elizabeth, is with Miss Kilman, her history tutor.

The narrative now shifts to Elizabeth and Miss Kilman. They go to tea in a department store, and Elizabeth sets out on her own for a bus ride and a short walk before she returns home to ready for the party that evening.

Septimus and Lucrezia, by this time, have returned home to pass the afternoon in their apartment. Dr. Holmes, a doctor Septimus dreads, forces his way inside. Septimus's madness and his horror of doctors' control over him leads him to jump from the apartment window to his death.

The sound of Septimus's ambulance is heard by Peter Walsh, who is on his way back to his hotel.

Section 8

Clarissa's party is beginning; guests are arriving. Clarissa is experiencing anxiety, convinced that her party will be a failure. But it seems to be a success, and she makes the rounds of her guests. Sally Seton arrives, surprising Clarissa because Clarissa is not aware that Sally is in London from the country. The Prime Minister shows up, making everybody feel very satisfied that they are such distinguished company. Sally and Peter chat and wait for Clarissa to mingle with others before she can visit with them. Finally, guests begin to leave. Richard goes to join his daughter, and Clarissa goes to talk to her old friends. Upon seeing Clarissa move toward him, Peter feels great pleasure that this event has ended his day.

Dr. Bradshaw

See Sir William Bradshaw

Sir William Bradshaw

While Dr. Bradshaw, unlike Dr. Holmes, immediately grasps the gravity and nature of Septimus's condition, he is still not a likable character. He seems very similar to Dr. Holmes. The book's argument against these doctors is that they are primarily concerned with managing individual cases of social and psychological distress without being interested in the causes of such problems. Thus, these doctors are still a part of the problem. They help to maintain the status quo by smoothing over difficulties instead of approaching psychological disturbance as evidence of deep social problems that must be addressed.

Lady Bruton

Lady Bruton is the character with whom Richard Dalloway and Hugh Whitbread have lunch. She is a woman of strong character and active in public and political life. She always uses her influence in matters about which she feels strongly. Her new interest is in emigration, that is, encouraging young British couples to emigrate to Canada, one of the British Commonwealth countries. She asks Richard and Hugh to revise her letter to the editorial section of the major London newspaper, the *Times*, the forum in which she plans to air her views.

Daisy

Daisy is referred to in passing as the woman whom Peter Walsh is to marry. Peter is in London arranging matters for her divorce, among other business, as she is presently married.

Clarissa Dalloway

Clarissa Dalloway is the principal character of *Mrs. Dalloway,* since it is her party that gives definition to the narrative and her point of view dominates the book. She was born Clarissa Parry, and the day the novel takes place, she is approximately fifty years old. Her husband is Richard Dalloway, and they have one child, Elizabeth. The overwhelming impression Clarissa gives is that she is a solitary, even isolated, being, and that she is often consumed with thoughts or feelings of death and mortality. This is not only because her thoughts of friends are for those of her youth and not present ones, but also because she seems to desire isolation. She chooses Richard Dalloway over Peter Walsh as a husband not because she loves him more, but because she believes Richard will not consume all of her personality and time, or all of her emotional and intellectual reserves. Clarissa sleeps in her own room, in a small single bed that is likened to a coffin, and such suggestions and imagery of isolation and death surround her throughout the book.

The reader gains a sense of Clarissa's character both from her own thoughts and from what other characters, especially Peter, think about her. Besides the fact that she has inspired love, which speaks well of her, she is also someone whom others, and herself, think flawed. Peter's notion that she is the "perfect hostess" sums up this suspicion of her weakness. Clarissa is well-off and does not work, putting her in a position to cultivate her preferences, which are the pursuits of beauty and social harmony. While she knows that these are worthy pursuits, she and her friends nevertheless wonder whether this is a wholly ethical way to live. The question she and they ask is whether or not she should be more like her husband or Lady Bruton and take a more obviously practical role in public and political life.

Elizabeth Dalloway

Elizabeth Dalloway is Clarissa's daughter. She is just coming of age, and she is somewhat in the thrall of her history tutor, Doris Kilman. However, Elizabeth is also her own person. When she goes out on a shopping trip with Miss Kilman, she soon parts from her tutor and steals a few hours to be by herself before she must return home to get ready for her mother's party.

Richard Dalloway

Richard Dalloway, despite being Clarissa's husband, does not play a large role in the novel. He was not as close to Clarissa as Peter and Sally were during their youthful days. Rather, in the various characters' memories of their mutual past, Richard is a late arrival on the youthful scene. He arrives around the time Clarissa is thinking about marriage and presents himself as the perfect husband for her, in contrast to Peter. He is a politician and member of Parliament and the Conservative Party, demonstrating Clarissa's and his relative social and political conservatism, especially compared to Peter and Sally.

Ellie Henderson

Ellie is Clarissa's cousin, whom Clarissa invites to her party at the last minute at the request of a mutual acquaintance. Ellie is not well-off and gets out very seldom, so she is grateful to have the opportunity to attend such an exciting affair.

Dr. Holmes

Dr. Holmes is an overbearing and controlling doctor who does not understand Septimus's condition and whose ignorance and arrogance do Septimus more harm than good. His arrival at

Septimus's apartment is the last straw for the young man. Rather than fall under Holmes's control, Septimus throws himself out of a window, killing himself.

Miss Doris Kilman

Doris Kilman is a single, educated woman to whom life has not been particularly kind or just. While she possessed employment of some security before the war, her refusal to jump on the war bandwagon and call all Germans enemies made her unpopular and caused her to be dismissed from her post. Left to fend for herself during the lean war years, she scrapes together a living from incidental tutoring and lecturing. She feels great bitterness about her misfortunes and develops a religious fanaticism that makes her extremely unpopular with Clarissa, who fears and resents the woman's influence on Elizabeth.

Lucy

Lucy is the principal housemaid in the Dalloway home, and she and the cook are primarily responsible for readying the house for the party.

Aunt Parry

See Miss Helena Parry

Media Adaptations

- *Mrs. Dalloway* was adapted into a film of the same name in 1997, directed by Marleen Gorris. It stars the venerated British actor Vanessa Redgrave as Clarissa Dalloway.

Miss Helena Parry

Clarissa's aunt is a minor character in the book. She figures early on as the relative at Bourton whom the younger people seem to enjoy shocking. She surprises Peter at the end of the book by still being alive and by being present at the party.

Sylvia Parry

Sylvia, Clarissa's sister, is only mentioned in

passing, but is significant nevertheless. She was killed by a falling tree at Bourton. The name "Sylvia" is Latinate, meaning "wild" or "woods." Her death signifies the death of youth and freedom, as Clarissa's freedom and youth ended at Bourton when she decided to marry. That is, her life since Bourton has been one in which she is not so much her own person as Richard's wife.

Rezia

See Lucrezia Warren Smith

Lady Rosseter

See Sally Seton

Sally Seton

Sally, with Peter and Clarissa, was a member of the close triangle of friends who often spent time together at Bourton. Sally delighted her friends with her vibrant personality and her legendary exploits. Clarissa was so taken by Sally that she fell in love with her, as she realizes years later. Sally, like Clarissa, went on to marry, marrying a self-made man whose success eventually earns him high social distinction, giving Sally the title "Lady Rosseter."

Lucrezia Warren Smith

Lucrezia, or Rezia, is Septimus's wife. He met her in Italy where he was stationed for part of WWI, as Italy was one of Britain's allies during the war. While she was happy to marry Septimus and set out to a foreign country, now in London she is in despair because Septimus is no longer the same man she married. His war trauma is now deep-seated and advanced and she finds herself alone and confused about what is happening to her husband.

Septimus Warren Smith

After Clarissa, Septimus is the character of most importance. His story parallels Clarissa's to a certain extent, as both characters are radically isolated and seem at odds with prevailing forces in the world. Septimus came to London as a young man in search of a career, and he showed early promise. He was an excellent worker interested in furthering his education, but then he went off to war. He returned from the war having fought bravely, but also with shell shock, a condition little understood at the time. He and his wife first seek help from a general practitioner, instead of immediately consulting the psychological specialist, Dr. Bradshaw, demonstrating people's unfamiliarity with mental disease and how to manage it at the time. Septimus is a portrait of a distressed mind, going through the hours of his last day, entertaining delusional thoughts and experiencing hallucinations, and ultimately, killing himself.

Peter Walsh

Peter Walsh is an Anglo-Indian, that is, a

British citizen who worked in India during Britain's administrative colonial control of that country. At the time of the book's events, he is visiting London. Peter is defined mostly by his having been deeply in love with Clarissa Dalloway and by his intention, during his youth, to marrying her. In fact, he still seems to be in love with her, despite having married after she rejected him, and despite the fact that he is planning to marry for a second time. Of the group of close, youthful friends, Sally, Clarissa and himself, he seems more like Sally than like Clarissa. Sally and Peter were very lively; they took chances and espoused forward-looking political and social views.

Hugh Whitbread

Hugh Whitbread is deemed by most characters in the book (Peter, Sally, Richard) to be dull and uninteresting. There is the sense that he is a little ridiculous and quite conventional. Clarissa has the most sympathy for him as she appreciates his good qualities. Foremost amongst his good points are his loyalty and obedience. He always tried to please his mother and he looks after his ailing and fragile wife, Evelyn, dutifully.

Consciousness

Although it is difficult to imagine, the novel is a relatively new literary form. Poetry and drama (plays), for example, have a much longer history. The novel, however, did not arise as a unique genre until the late eighteenth century. According to literary historians, it arose along with, or partly because of, the rise of the individual.

It is said that Woolf's style, and that of other early-twentieth-century novelists, represents a culmination of this connection between the novel and the individual. Before there were "individuals," so to speak, a person lived his or her life according to what was determined from the outside or according to what society decreed was correct. A person did not go through life assuming that he or she could make personal, or individual, decisions and choices. The literary historians argue, then, that when this new type of person, this "individual," began to exist, it needed new literary forms to express itself. The novel was one of these forms.

What comes with being an individual is a sense of separateness and uniqueness, a sense of being apart. One way this sense of being separate is cultivated is by each person focusing on, or developing a sense of, his or her own mind or consciousness. The novel is a literary form of the individual, literary historians argue, because novelists present and explore characters who have significant interior lives.

In novels such as *Mrs. Dalloway*, consciousness and an internal life are central preoccupations. *Mrs. Dalloway* is largely made up of the internal thoughts of its various characters. It is for this reason that novels like *Mrs. Dalloway* represent a culmination of an historical process of individuation. Preceding novels had not so intensively focused on the interior life of characters, or on what characters thought to themselves. That is, the characters in *Mrs. Dalloway* and similar novels are featured as individual thinkers even more than they are presented as persons interacting socially with others. It is the characters' individual qualities that are highlighted.

In a sense, the character of Clarissa Dalloway is a representation of extreme, problematic individualism, in that she recognizes her absolute isolation. She is distant from her husband, she appears to have few current friends, and she secludes herself in her own small room as if she were a quiet nun in a convent or a solitary prisoner in a cell. The reader derives this sense of an absolutely isolated consciousness when, for instance, Clarissa watches the old woman across the way. Unseen, looking out from the window of her solitary chamber, separated from the woman by walls and distance, Clarissa seems trapped within the confines of her own consciousness.

The novel seems to ask if people can truly

communicate and connect if each is enclosed within his or her own consciousness. Whether the novel resolves this issue, or merely explores it, is for each reader to decide. Is Clarissa's party evidence of true communion between people despite separateness? Does the imagery of waves and connecting threads and webs complicate the imagery of isolation? Do the depictions of shared public sights and sounds indicate fully shared experience, or simply common experience differently understood?

Social Change

Some critics believe that *Mrs. Dalloway* is an apolitical and an asocial novel about individual internal life as opposed to social life. Others insist that the political and social context of the time is included in the book and important to its events. Critics who believe the novel is concerned with social and political events and developments of the time, consider it a novel of suggestion, not argumentation. Woolf dropped hints and touched lightly on social and political developments, they say, and a discerning reader is able to make out intended meanings from the author's allusions.

For example, WWI is obviously important to the sense of the novel. It is what ruins Septimus's life and career and what hounds him to his death.

Additionally, the histories of Septimus and Dr. Bradshaw indicate that classism is on the wane in the Britain of *Mrs. Dalloway*. Whereas a person's social class determined his or her possibilities in earlier days, now Bradshaw has risen from humble circumstances to greatness, having earned a title (he is *Sir* William Bradshaw). Similarly, the lower-middle-class Septimus, before the war, was on his way to a brilliant career and upward social mobility.

Topics for Further Study

- Research shell shock in relation to WWI. How do treatments for war trauma today differ from those used then?

- What was the role of women during WWI? How did women contribute to the war effort in Britain?

The reader also learns that the political and social scene of Britain is changing significantly, as details of the rise of the Labour Party and of unrest in India are revealed. These details indicate the shifting of political power to the party that represents the interests of the broadest population, instead of remaining faithful to the interests of the old, aristocratic ruling classes. It also shows non-European nations beginning to agitate for freedom from foreign intervention and control.

Also significantly, Elizabeth Dalloway's rumination over a career indicates how the education of young women and their social positions are changing. As opposed to only having indirect influence through their husbands, like Lady Bruton, young women like Elizabeth can have public careers in their own right. Thus, *Mrs. Dalloway* stays true to Woolf's assertion, expressed in her essay "Mr. Bennett and Mrs. Brown," that, around 1910, human character and society changed: "All human relations have shifted—those between masters and servants, husbands and wives, parents and children. And when human relations change there is at the same time a change in religion, conduct, politics, and literature." In short, those persons and classes traditionally without social or cultural power appear in *Mrs. Dalloway* as coming into a position to exercise their rights, to have appreciable social influence, and to achieve upward social mobility.

Style

Narration and Point of View

From the very first sentence, *Mrs. Dalloway* shows the secure meshing of a third person (external) narrator's point of view with a first person, character's point of view, such that it is not possible to separate or distinguish the two: "Mrs. Dalloway said she would buy the flowers herself." If the two had been clearly separated the sentence would read: "Mrs. Dalloway said, 'I will buy the flowers myself'," or would have included the word "that": "Mrs. Dalloway said *that* she would buy the flowers herself." In this second case, the reader would assume that the words following the word "that" were not necessarily faithful to Mrs. Dalloway's thought or speech, but rather that they are a narrator's interpretation or summary. Instead, what Woolf perfected in this novel is a style of narration that literary critics have called "represented thought and speech," capturing the motions of a mind thinking in the past tense, third person. A narrator presents character thought and speech, but the narrator's words are wholly and immediately imbued by the voice and style of the particular character in question; there is no way to separate narrator and character. Woolf invented an elegant and efficient way of moving between and representing multiple characters' speech and thought; the clumsiness of excessive dialogue or of switching between sequences of different characters' thoughts presented in the first person is avoided. Related terms in literary criticism are re-ported thought and speech, free indirect discourse, and stream-of-consciousness.

Time

Mrs. Dalloway is striking for the way that its events occur within a single day. This unusual strategy announces the novel's complication of time in general. For example, while most people tend to think of time in terms of the regular clicking away of the clock—of seconds, minutes, hours, and days—this book shows how people can relive, through the operations of memory, whole years within the space of minutes. Peter and Clarissa walk a few paces in London and remember major periods of their youth, how these years affected them, and how they shaped their lives.

On a related theme, the novel multiplies time by presenting the thoughts of myriad characters, each of whom remember and experience time, the past and the present, in different ways. In this novel, chronological time is only one sense of time, as the characters bring the past into the present, allow the meaning and remembrance of the present to be shaped by the past, and shape memories of and feelings about the past with experience in the present.

Character Double

Septimus Warren Smith can be seen as Clarissa's double in the novel. As a character double, he is a character whose attributes and story fill out the character and story of Clarissa. According to the literary critic Alex Page, in "A Dangerous Day: Mrs. Dalloway and Her Double," "Septimus's character is in all essentials Clarissa's, but taken to a deadly extreme." Where Clarissa is isolated, Septimus is disassociated from reality; where Clarissa manages the disappointments and strictures society imposes upon her, Septimus buckles under greater pressures. The close connections of these characters is made clear by Clarissa's deep upset when Dr. Bradshaw informs her, at her party, that one of his patients committed suicide that day. She retreats from her guests in shock when Bradshaw mentions Septimus's death, as if she herself were susceptible to the same degree of despair that destroys the young man.

The New Modern Era

The nineteenth century ushered in developments that profoundly changed European society. Mercantilism and industrialism created a powerful new class. The cultural, political and economic might of this new class, the bourgeoisie or middle-class, soon overtook that of the aristocratic classes that had controlled nations and empires before. The spread of democracy and workers' rights movements also characterized the nineteenth century. It was not until after World War I (1914–1918), however, that a deep sense of how extremely and permanently European society had changed prevailed.

Mrs. Dalloway registers this sense of the end of an era. Clarissa's Aunt Parry, the aged relic who makes an appearance at Clarissa's party, represents this decline and this ending of an old way of life. The old woman likes to remember her days in Burma, a time and place suggestive of the height of British imperialism and colonialism. But, as Lady Bruton's distressed comment about the situation in India makes clear, the old days of paternalistic European colonialism are over. India and other colonies that used to be comfortable homes for colonials like Clarissa's aunt are now uncomfortable places where the beginnings of serious battles for independence are occurring.

Lady Bruton also mentions the Labour Party's ascendancy. (This new party gained a parliamentary majority in England in 1924, the year before *Mrs. Dalloway* was published.) This detail indicates how the England of this time had become radically modern in its move to a fuller social democracy, the political system that still characterizes most modern nations today, including the United States. The Labour Party's name indicates its representation of rule by the people, for the people, as opposed to rule by an aristocracy or an oligarchic class.

Elizabeth Dalloway, a young woman considering a career, is also an indicator of change, as entering the working world was a social possibility not available to women before this time.

Compare & Contrast

- **1920s:** In Britain, the Labour Party rises to power, women get the right to vote, and the first major wave of communication and travel tech nologies are incipient or, in some cases, widely established (radio, telephone, telegraph commu nications; automobile and airplane travel).

  Today: International communications and connections have progressed to such an extent, due to computer technology and the

Internet, that the term "globalization" is in common use. The modern world foreseen in the 1920s has definitively arrived.

- **1920s:** Modernism, the set of artistic move ments that try to express, through form and style, the cultural and social changes of a brand new century, is flourishing. The modernists profess internationalism. **Today:** Art at the close of the twentieth century is defined by postmodernism. The name of this new set of movements suggests how its forms are both tied to modernism (post*modernism*), and in some ways defined against modernism (*post*modernism). Postmodernists examine and question globalization and transnationalism.

- **1920s:** While the American colonies of Europe (i.e., the United States and the nations of South and Central America) have long since established themselves as independent nations, the twentieth century is characterized by nationalist and independence movements in Europe's remaining colonies (in Asia and Africa). These movements are not brought to a close until the 1960s.

Today: Colonies no longer exist; rather, a group of independent nations cover the globe.

WWI

WWI bears comparison with the Vietnam War. Like this more recent war, it is remembered as a war that many thought should have been avoided and that traumatized its soldiers. It was an imperial war in two senses. First, it was an attempt to limit the European encroachments of Prussian imperial rule and power. Second, it was partially provoked by border skirmishes among European nations on the African continent (European nations had begun colonizing African territories in the late nineteenth century). It was a power struggle pertaining to traditional European ruling classes and had very little to do with the everyday concerns and struggles of most European citizens.

What was shocking about the war was how long it dragged on and how many casualties it produced. (It lasted four years and millions of young men died or were terribly wounded.) The style of fighting developed in this war was trench warfare. In trench warfare, soldiers dig deep ditches from which they shoot at the enemy. When given the order to charge, they climb out of these trenches and meet the enemy head-on. These cramped, claustrophobic trenches were breeding grounds for disease, as they were muddy and wet from frequent rainfall. Soldiers felt that the trenches were as much ready-made earthly graves as they were protection from enemy fire. Also, poison gas (mustard gas) was used during WWI, and soldiers caught by the fumes without gas masks died or suffered horribly.

Enemy soldiers often formed friendships during cease-fire periods in the space of no man's land between opposing trench lines. Soldiers on both sides felt strongly that their real enemies were not each other, but the officers, politicians and generals who were running the war. The carnage, mutilation, and terror of this badly managed war resulted in a host of traumatized war veterans. This trauma was given the name "shell shock" in the years following the war. Septimus Warren Smith, who was a brave soldier, but who ends up a suicidal, ruined man, indicates Woolf's condemnation of this unfortunate war.

Critical Overview

All of Woolf's publications, fictional and non-fictional alike, have received a great deal of critical attention. A bibliography of criticism on Woolf would be a very hefty book in its own right, as her work has been the subject of intense study since she began writing, and it is still a major topic today. Considered equal to the likes of Shakespeare, James Joyce, and Charlotte Brontë, Virginia Woolf is indisputably one of the English language's greatest literary voices.

Major topics in the criticism on *Mrs. Dalloway* are the significance of Clarissa's party as the culminating event of the book, and Peter Walsh's and others' criticism of her parties. At one point in the novel, Clarissa is plagued by a bad feeling. With some thought, she arrives at the source of her anxiety: "Her parties! That was it! Her parties! Both of them [Peter and Richard] criticised her very unfairly, laughed at her unjustly for her parties. That was it! That was it!" She goes on to think: "Well, how was she going to defend herself?"

Critics have defended Clarissa amply by theorizing the significance of the opposition of Richard, parliamentarian and politician, and the seemingly apolitical, spoilt Clarissa, giver of parties and lover of beauty. For Suzette A. Henke, in "*Mrs. Dalloway:* the Communion of Saints," Clarissa's party is akin to a sacred mass, "a ritual culminating in sacred communion." In the opinion of Jeremy Hawthorn, in *Virginia Woolf's "Mrs. Dalloway": A Study in Alienation*, the party "is not just Clarissa's gift, it is the occasion for communal giving ... which will recharge the participants' social sense and ... allow them temporarily to escape from their alienated selves."

Other critics, along these lines, suggest Woolf's book argues that politicians like Richard would not be so busy cleaning up the messes of the world if people were brought up to love harmony, communication, community, and beauty before all other things. It is not, then, that *Mrs. Dalloway* is an apolitical or anti-political novel, these critics argue, but rather that its politics are radically different from the norm—the book advances a politic of beauty and community, as it were.

Many feminist critics suggest that this opposition of political styles is a gender issue. To these critics, it seems that Woolf understands that traditional women's work (mothering children, maintaining family bonds) emphasizes social bonding over competition. Women, therefore, and books like *Mrs. Dalloway*, have important lessons for society at large, and suggest how it might function more smoothly.

Related to considerations about the significance of Clarissa's parties are estimations about the novel's connection to contemporaneous social and political events. Until perhaps the last twenty years of Woolf criticism, a prevailing view was that Woolf was not at all interested in the "real world." The novelist E. M. Forster, Woolf's famous contemporary, stated in his book *Virginia Woolf* that "improving the world she [Woolf] would not consider" was not her intention. Yet, as other critics point out, such an opinion does not hold up when the author's own diary records that the novel's purpose was "to criticise the social system, & show it at work, at its most intense." (This entry concerning *Mrs. Dalloway* can be found in Vol. II of *The Diary of Virginia Woolf*.)

Critics who examine this aspect of the novel discuss Woolf's subtle, if not wholesale, indictment of the outdated and overly conservative attitudes of Richard, Lady Bruton, and Hugh, and argue that the suffering of Septimus is to be understood as the result of such problematic views and policies. The prevailing attitude today concerning the book's politics, and Woolf's social views in general, is expressed succinctly by Suzette A. Henke (in the article previously cited): "All of Virginia Woolf's major novels suggest an intellectual commitment to feminist, pacifist, and socialist principles."

Another topic in the criticism of *Mrs. Dalloway* is an examination of Septimus and Clarissa as problems in psychology and mental health. Knowing that Woolf herself suffered bouts of mental disease, they find these characters' portraits a wealth of information. Another significant body of criticism focuses on questions of sexuality in the novel, considering, for example, Clarissa's love for Sally Seton. Some critics suggest that Clarissa's extreme feelings of isolation are to be understood partly as the result of a deleteriously suppressed homosexuality. In "Clarissa Dalloway's Respectable Suicide," Emily Jensen expresses this view: "No simple girlhood crush, Clarissa's love for Sally Se-ton is a profound reality that permeates her adult life." This critic goes on to say that Clarissa's suppression of this love is a sort of suicide, a death in life, "on a par with Septimus Smith's more obvious suicide." Jensen approaches Septimus as Clarissa's double, that is, as a character who aids the reader in arriving at a fuller understanding of Clarissa. Jensen's essay, in this way, intersects with yet another significant set of inquiries into the novel, which considers the book's clusters of characters, especially the clustering or doubling of Septimus and Clarissa.

What Do I Read Next?

- *To the Lighthouse* (1927) was Woolf's next novel, after the success of *Mrs. Dalloway*. It concerns a large family spending a summer at the seaside, much like Woolf's own family did during her childhood.

- *Ulysses* (1922), by James Joyce, is a challenging book. The title refers to the famous classical Greek story of a man's epic travels (those of Odysseus, also called Ulysses). The epic journey, it has been said, refers less to the main character's (Ulysses'/Leopold Bloom's) perambulations through Dublin and more to the journey the reader experiences as he or she reads through the extraordinary stylistic shifts that make up this modernist novel. Like *Mrs. Dalloway, Ulysses* takes place within a single day and characterizes a city as well as its characters.

- *The Hours* (1998), by Michael Cunningham, is a recently published novel based on Woolf's *Mrs. Dalloway*. It interweaves the lives of three women in three times: Virginia Woolf in 1923, a 1949 Woolf fan in Los Angeles, and a present day Clarissa, planning a party.

- *The Sound and the Fury* (1929), by William Faulkner, is a novel whose stylistic beauty and experimentation represent an American modernism contemporaneous to the experiments of Virginia Woolf and James Joyce abroad.

Sources

Forster, E. M., *Aspects of the Novel*, Harcourt, Brace & Co., 1927.

—————————, *Virginia Woolf*, Cambridge University Press, 1942.

Hawthorn, Jeremy, *Virginia Woolf's "Mrs. Dalloway": A Study in Alienation*, Sussex University Press, 1975.

Henke, Suzette A., *"Mrs. Dalloway:* the Communion of Saints," in *New Feminist Essays on Virginia Woolf*, edited by Jane Marcus, University of Nebraska Press, 1981, pp. 125-47.

Jensen, Emily, "Clarissa Dalloway's Respectable Suicide," in *Virginia Woolf: A Feminist Slant*, edited by Jane Marcus, University of Nebraska Press, 1983, pp. 162-79.

Page, Alex, "A Dangerous Day: Mrs. Dalloway and Her Double," in *Modern Fiction Studies*, Vol. VII, No. 2, Summer 1961, pp. 115-24.

Woolf, Virginia, *The Diary of Virginia Woolf*, edited by Anne Olivier Bell with Andrew McNeillie, 5 vols., Hogarth Press, 1977–1984.

—————————, "Mr. Bennett and Mrs. Brown," in *The Gender of Modernism*, edited by Bonnie Kime Scott, Indiana University Press, 1990.

For Further Study

Abel, Elizabeth, *Virginia Woolf and the Fictions of Psychoanalysis*, University of Chicago Press, 1989.

> The brilliant chapter on *Mrs. Dalloway* from Abel's book examines the way in which Woolf's novel responds to and contests Freud's theories about women.

Daiches, David, *Virginia Woolf*, James Laughlin, 1942.

> Daiches book gives an excellent, highly readable overview of Woolf's art and fictions.

Edwards, Lee R., "War and Roses: The Politics of *Mrs. Dalloway,*" in *The Authority of Experience: Essays in Feminist Criticism*, edited by Arlyn Diamond and Lee R. Edwards, University of Massachusetts Press, 1977, pp. 161-77.

> This essay provides an important and informative aspect on the politics of *Mrs. Dalloway*.

Fussell, Paul, *The Great War and Modern Memory*, Oxford University Press, 1975.

> Fussel's text is a definitive book on WWI—its life in the popular imagination, the way soldiers experienced it, and the poetry of its

soldiers.

Lee, Hermione, *Virginia Woolf*, Alfred A. Knopf, Inc., 1996.

> Lee presents a recent and highly readable biography of the author.

Thomas, Sue, "Virginia Woolf's Septimus Smith and Contemporary Perceptions of Shellshock," in *English Language Notes*, Vol. 25, No. 2, December 1987, pp. 49-57.

> Thomas offers an examination of the literature and attitudes about shell shock in Woolf's time.

Zwerdling, Alex, *Virginia Woolf and the Real World*, University of California Press, 1986.

> Zwerdling's book discusses the social and political contexts and arguments of Woolf's novels.

Lightning Source UK Ltd.
Milton Keynes UK
UKHW02f1849250918
329518UK00016B/1002/P